THE *Wishing* TOWEL

---·◦◆◦·---

THE ROSE COLLECTION

CHERYL A. HYMON

Copyright © 2022 Cheryl A. Hymon.

All rights reserved. No part of this book may be reproduced, stored, or transmitted by any means—whether auditory, graphic, mechanical, or electronic—without written permission of both publisher and author, except in the case of brief excerpts used in critical articles and reviews. Unauthorized reproduction of any part of this work is illegal and is punishable by law.

ISBN: 979-8-88640-316-9 (sc)
ISBN: 979-8-88640-317-6 (hc)
ISBN: 979-8-88640-318-3 (e)

Because of the dynamic nature of the Internet, any web addresses or links contained in this book may have changed since publication and may no longer be valid. The views expressed in this work are solely those of the author and do not necessarily reflect the views of the publisher, and the publisher hereby disclaims any responsibility for them.

One Galleria Blvd., Suite 1900, Metairie, LA 70001
1-888-421-2397

Contents

Acknowledgements 1
Foreword 3
He Came For Me 5
The Rose 8
The Rose Vision 9
Heaven Sent 10
Dancer 11
Christian's Journey 12
Sting of Death 13
Forsake Not! 14
Appointed Season 17
Heaven's Gates 20
Arm of the Lord 21
Wandering in Darkness 22
Spirit of the Lord 23
Turning of the Wall 24
Whisper of the Wind 25
Free at Last 26
The Prize 27
Crack in the Window 28
Henrietta and Monica 29
At the Sound of the Trumpet 30
Alice 31
Tears 32
Miracle Over the Mountain 33
The Golden Rainbow 34
Emerald Pools 35
He Talked to Me Today 36
Thy Heart's Cry 37
To Someone 38
Songbird 39
Kiss 40

Coffee, Tea or Me	41
Scratch My Wings	42
The Sandy Rose	43
New Day Dawning	44
The Late Night Watchman	45
The Jewel's Vine	46
Precious Jewels to Behold	47
My Tablet	48
God's Blueprint	49
Flecks of Gold	50
He is the Cornerstone	51
Breath of Heaven	52
For Such a Time as This	53
Seek His Face	54
The Spirit's Blessing	55
Step by Step	56
Valley of Peace	57
Silent Smile	58
I Am With You in Spirit	59
The Uncertainties in Witnessing	60
Nothing Can Keep Me Down	61
City Lights	62
Embrace Me	63
Turning Your Home Into a Fortress	64
Middle of the Road	65
Birthday Present	67
Majestic Beauty	68
Hiding Place	69
Out of Prayer	70
In Prayer	73
The Master's Touch	74
Draw from the Fountain	75
Express One's Gratitude	76
Fragranced Home	77
Protection Bottle	78
About the Author	79

Acknowledgements

Loving Support of my husband, Rick Hymon.
Carla Duncan: My friend, and faithful intercessor.
Donna Walker: Your unending encouragement. Susan Soto:
Thank you for your diligence in prayer and editing.
Family and friends: Your prayers and encouraging words.
Most of All: Jesus, The Divine Writer.

Foreword

On June 26, 1990 during a time of study, I penciled three names in my journal: Asaph, Heman and Jeduthun. I didn't have a clue what it meant. Later as my daughter and I were attending a dance class, The Lord spoke to me saying, "A woman here will have something to tell you today" and He revealed the woman. Well three hours later the class ended and as we were walking in the parking lot, the woman turned around and began to speak to me. She told me that I would be writing poetry, songs and narrative writings.

The Lord inspired the first poem, *'The Rose'* just three weeks later. As The Lord gave me the words, I could smell a wonderful fragrance. At the time, no one else was in the room! The excitement and hungry anticipation began that morning. Poetic writing inspired by The Lord was always meant to be an encouragement and it truly has been.

The poems in this collection were birthed to encourage the reader. This collection is filled with day-to-day experiences and with God's never-leave-nor-forsake provision. In preparation for the publication of *'The Wishing Towel'*, I felt renewed, my cup being filled up again, full of joy and focused on Jesus.

When Jesus was on earth He took a cloth from His Girdle and washed the Disciples' feet. They did not understand. Likewise, we also do not understand 'the washing process'. Sometimes we are in the wilderness, sometimes on the mountaintop, sometimes in the valley. We find ourselves wishing or hoping for better tomorrows.

Don't throw in your towel.
Let God's Towel wash away
All the hurts,
The disappointments,
And sorrow.
He knows how much we can bear and He is our Buckler.
As a memorial, He will place jewels in our breastplate.
Our alabaster box will break open
With Praises to His Glorious Name.

He Came For Me

The Samaritans and the Jews had had nothing to do with each other for 700 years. A certain man had the Samaritans exiled and then foreigners moved into the area and married the people in the city. The Jews were biased against the Samaritans treating them as 'outcasts' because they had married foreigners. Jesus is not biased. He came to the earth to reveal the Truth and life about God.

A Universal Parable: And then one day, Jesus took a short route through Samaria. He came to a city in Samaria called Sychar and Jacob's Well was there. His disciples had gone into the city to buy food. As He had tired from His journey, He sat down by the well. A Samaritan woman came to draw water into her waterpot and Jesus asked her to give Him a drink. She stated, *"Why are you talking to me as I am a Samaritan woman and you are a Jew and they have no dealings with Samaritans?"* He told her that if she drank from the water that He could provide she would thirst no more. Jesus asked her to call her husband to come here. She stated that she did not have a husband. Jesus said, *"You have spoken well as you have had five husbands and the one you are now with is not your husband."* She perceived Him to be a Prophet as He knew all about her. She then talked to Jesus about her place of worship and the Jews place of worship and Jesus replied, *"Woman, believe Me, the hour is coming when you will neither on this mountain, nor in Jerusalem, worship the Father. You worship what you do not know; we know what we worship for salvation is of the Jews. But the hour is coming, and now is, when the true worshippers will worship The Father in spirit and truth for the Father is seeking such to worship Him. God is Spirit, and those who worship Him must worship in spirit and truth."* The woman stated, *"I know that the Messiah is coming who is called Christ. When He comes, He will tell us all things."* Jesus said to her, *"I who speak to you am He."*

At this point, His disciples came and they marveled that He talked with a woman; yet no one said, "What do you seek?" or, "Why are you talking with her?" The woman received what He had said to her, leaving her waterpot, and she ran to tell the men of the city. She ran is an expression of excitement and joy that a person experiences when they first meet Jesus. She was received as telling the Truth and many of the Samaritans of that city believed in Him because of the word of the woman who testified, *"He told me all that I ever did."* So when the Samaritans had come to Him, they urged Him to stay with them and He stayed there two days. And many more believed because of His own word.

The Samaritan woman had gone to draw water into her waterpot many, many times, which was hard manual labor. But on this appointed day, she was at the right place at the right time. She found Jesus sitting by the well. She expressed to Jesus that she did not understand why He was speaking to her because of their differences. Her day-to-day journey, religious posture as she knew it, was about to be miraculously and marvelously changed. Jesus told her that if she would receive Him as Christ, she would thirst no more; fountains of living water would flow into her life. She couldn't contain herself as that day The Lord was constrained to sup with her, to reverse her situation, to break hell wide open, to give her Life. No more toil but now leaning on His Everlasting Arms. Her name was not mentioned but this parable is a memorial to her. Jesus knew everything about her. He knew her destiny. He knew about the plan. He knew about the purpose. She was the key! She lived in a very treacherous time.

Also the Jews would sing a song that goes like this: It is better to be a man than a woman ……….. So the Samaritan woman already had low self-esteem with people treating her as an outcast. She had lived a life of religion and now she had accepted Jesus as her personal savior. This was an appointed time for her. A personal conversation with Jesus and everything that was promised, she would now receive. A turning from the old life, the life of sorrow, uncertainty and toil to a life full of joy, truth and life. Jacob's well was a place of promise. Jesus will meet you in a very special way.

Jesus is a King who sits High
And looks low, a True Servant,
Willing to wash our feet with His Towel.

If we Seek, Go and Follow Him,
He will wash away our hurts, our tears,
Our disappointments, our failures and
Most of all, He will fill us with Himself.
Whatever was not clear will become crystal clear.
Whatever we did not understand, He will help us to understand.

He will give us the desires of our heart.

Take a moment to ask Jesus to come into your heart.
Receive Him with gladness
And come before His Presence with singing as
He Came For You!

John 4: 1-45

The Rose

Ye are the Rose of Sharon
The Lily of the Valley,
Ye are the Great Magnificent One
Ye are all these things wrapped into one,
Ye are the Bright Morning Star
Ye are the Radiant Light
That has shown on us so bright.
Your fragrance is like a flower
And it permeates so sweet
We long for the day that we shall meet.
Your outreached hand ever so gently touches
To deliver us from the fiery pit
In order that your call
On our lives may fit.
We long to embrace our Heavenly Father
For You are our light by day
And our light by night.
Grateful are we that we will fly
Upon your outreached wings
And shall forever
Sing praises to our King.

John 12:3

*Then Mary took a pound of very costly
Oil of spikenard,
Anointed the feet of Jesus
And wiped His feet with her hair.
And the house was filled
With the fragrance of the oil.*

The Rose Vision

In a Vision, The Lord revealed to me that I was like a long stemmed red rose, the petals of the perfect rose so soft, beautiful, perfected but as you go up the stem there are "thorns". He said He would remove the thorns. We are not to get upset with ourselves because we do not do everything right because He sees us differently.

My children's Great Grandmother had stomach cancer and had been out of her coma approximately 24 hours when the kids and I went to see her. In the course of talking to her, I told her about my vision. She closed her eyes as though The Spirit had quickened in her, reopened her eyes and began to tell me what she had seen while she was in a coma. She had a dream that she was a yellow rose and that her right hand was a petal from her thumb to her little finger. She stated that I was to pray with her and she would be complete to go to be with The Lord.

Then she explained how in the winter time a child might go into the woods and pick what seems to be a dead stem or weed and as you begin to poke at it you are aware that there is still some green to it—some life.

Then she said, *"Pray on it, pray on it,"* meaning her right hand and I prayed with her and I felt The Holy Spirit move in her hand. The Lord took her to be with Him two days later. She was a miracle of God because even though she had stomach cancer she never had any pain. She had walked with The Lord most of her life. Sometimes God places special people in your path and you may or may not know His Purpose.

PRAISE
THELORD
ALLYESAINTS

Heaven Sent

It is written
That the Lord shall provide
All the blessings needed
From Heaven on high
Our Heavenly Father
Has proclaimed
The Good News
That it is finished
And we shall be renewed.
Our Heavenly Father
Help us to pray
"Lord help us today"
Satan comes to devour
As we walk along the way.

Dancer

O, Graceful Dancer,
With such dedication
You praise Thee
As though you were following
An angel's steps
In seemingly effortless beauty
Anointed and appointed by Him
With skill and grace.
Stretch forth thy scepter
And lift up thy banner
For the God of Battles has gone out
Before His chosen instrument
To enlarge thy place
So as you hear the trumpets sounding
And the timbrels playing,
Rejoice in dance to the victory song
And *advance*
To the Mountain of The Lord

Christian's Journey

The growth of a child,
A Child of God,
Is a step-by-step process
Heeding the Word of God
Praying without ceasing
Guided
By all Truth
And enduring
All things.

Sting of Death

"A time to weep, … A time to mourn, … . ."
Where is Thy Sting?
O death is your name and fear is your game
As waves of grief pierce the loved ones
Who are weeping
Not knowing who to blame.
Our Blessed Savior
Will send Angels of Virtue to abide
With those who mourn
And they shall be comforted on every side.
No more worries, no more fears
No more sorrow, no more tears.
O Grave you cry out from the depths of the earth
Searching for victory
But you were swallowed up by Christ's Triumph
Just as a caterpillar blossoms into a colorful butterfly,
So are we changed freed from toil and sorrow
With no more questioning of tomorrow.
By the Brightness of His Rising
He shall be our Everlasting Light
And the days of mourning shall be ended.

Forsake Not!

On the Eve of Christmas, words CRIED from a dream "Someone in your family is going to die. Blessed are they who mourn for they shall be comforted on every side."

Waves of grief immediately pierced my heart. Lord, I can't say anything to my family. Lord, who? Tears gushed throughout the day. My family didn't know why I was crying—I couldn't tell them—my husband didn't understand—he left the house. I prayed throughout the day and sometime during that evening, the Lord revealed to me that it was one of my parents. Well, my Dad had been diagnosed with colon cancer and The Lord had revealed to me that he would not be healed. I immediately leaned to my own understanding and felt sure that it would be my Dad.

On December 29, I was at work and one of my co-workers stated that I had a phone call. I went to the phone and it was my mother's cousin delivering the news that my mother had committed suicide. Oh, Lord, it wasn't my Dad. It was my Mother. I cried so loud and all of my co-workers were so good to me. I worked with a Pastor's wife who laid hands on me and began to pray—I was numb—I was angry, why did she do this—I knew something was wrong but I didn't ever expect this. My Mother shot herself in the heart with a gun that my Dad had taught her to use for protection. No one was prepared for this tragedy. What happens to those who are left behind with unanswered questions. My Dad passed out at different times, he was totally helpless, someone else had to make the funeral arrangements, someone else had to drive him to the funeral. Over and over for one year after, my Dad kept rehearsing *"Why did she do it, why did she do it? Why!"*

My own children were devastated—angry—wanting to suppress it and couldn't—wondering if their Mother would do the same.

We all react differently so do not expect others to react as you have. Days passed and one Sunday morning as I was sitting in the sanctuary, I saw a beautiful Angel adorned in white coming toward me to minister and I felt the Touch of Virtue. Such Grace to behold. I have reflected many times remembering the words *"They shall be comforted on every side."* The Lord is faithful to His children — death is not pleasant at any time for any one.

HE IS FAITHFUL, HE IS FAITHFUL.

My parents had attended church until I reached the age of 11 and then by the Devil's stronghold, they stopped attending the sanctuary. Year after year melted away and no attempt was made towards returning until three or four months before my Mother's tragedy. During those years, problems did arise and the resolutions seemed to be long and drawn out. Not recognizing the spirits that they were dealing with, life offered disappointments. They watched their children grow up with emotional problems associated with anger, rejection, poor relationships and unforgiveness.

Well after one year, my Dad tried to go on with his life and we were able to talk about The Lord many times. He was reading his bible and attending the sanctuary. Then, his disease worsened and he was in pain all of the time. About six months later, he went on to be with The Lord, but not before he had expressed forgiveness to the loved ones in his life. My Dad was abused by his Father as a child, was in the Second World War and watched people being killed on each side of him, and then my Mother's death was just too much for him. After receiving the news of my Father's death, I grieved, but felt relieved that he could rest in peace now and didn't have any more pain. Shortly after my Father's death, The Lord came to me and said, *"Now I will be your Mother and Father."* I felt His Love in such a special way, as though I was sitting in His Lap and my desire was to stay.

Now all my brother and I had left was each other, but attempt after attempt left me with no response from my brother. He had walked away from the church and had become associated with a rough crowd. My brother became a drug user with a very expensive and deadly drug habit, heroine. He had two associates and was murdered by one of them. This twisted turn of events left me reflecting back on an experience in prayer. In March, 1991, The Lord said, *"I want you to lay before me for three nights."* Curiosity flashed before me as I said, *"Yes, Lord, I will. You have never asked me to do this before."* He is the Author and Finisher of our Faith. As I lay before The Lord, words were few and scattered. On the second night, deliverance came. My head and neck were shaking and I would ball up in a fetal position. I said, *"Lord, what are you doing?"* He said, *" I have come against the spirit of murder who has pursued you for a long time. (II Sam 7:1-9) I am beheading it, never to return again."* Even though I felt I understood, God revealed the full understanding in His Time. (II Sam 4:7-8)

As I grieved for my brother, The Lord walked with me "comforting me on every side." Three or four days after learning of my Brother's death, The Lord said, "You do not want revenge—you are not angry— you have no guilt—you do not blame Me—pray that when these two people are put in prison that they will accept Me." The police were saying that they felt that there were three people involved. I told them that I dreamt about two people. Later, it was revealed that there were only two people involved. Life lived in the fast lane can end before its time!

He will enlarge our steps as He goes before us directing our path. He is there in time of trouble or time of need, just open up the Bible and read. Read about David — a man after God's own heart.

Hebrews 10:25-27

Not forsaking the assembling of ourselves together, as the manner of some is; but exhorting one another; and so much the more, as Ye see the Day Approaching. For if we sin willfully after that we have received the Knowledge of The Truth, there remaineth no more sacrifice for sins, but a certain fearful looking for of judgment and fiery indignation, which shall devour the adversaries.

Appointed Season

A Child of Love was born to us one Blessed Day
Lying in a manger nestled in the hay
Born for One Reason in the Appointed Season.
God sent His Messenger Gabriel to announce to Mary
Unto You This Child is given, O Devout Woman
and you shall name Him Jesus.
He shall be Thy Light to the Gentiles
and Thy Glory of all God's People
and a sword shall pierce through Thy Soul
to reveal the thoughts of many hearts.
As the years passed, this Child of Love grew
stronger filled with wisdom
finding increased favor with God and man.
At age 12, his parents took him to the synagogue
as was the custom for the Year of the Passover.
He was taught by the Jewish teachers,
and in asking questions,
they were astonished at His Wisdom.
At Age 30, He was baptized by The Holy Spirit
and after His Return from Jordan He was led
By The Spirit into the wilderness
being tempted for 40 days by the devil.
Have you ever thought about
what Jesus experienced during the 40 days!
Until the 40 days had ended,
He did not eat and the devil then
showed Jesus all the kingdoms of the world
offering his power and glory to Him
if He would but worship him.
Jesus resisted the devil
answering him with the Word of God
and the devil after trying Him in every way
departed from Him for a SEASON.

After overcoming the devil, He began to preach
in a synagogue reading from Isaiah 61:1 these words:
The Spirit of the Sovereign Lord is on Me,
Because The Lord has anointed Me
To Preach Good News to the poor,
He has sent Me to proclaim freedom for the prisoners
and recovery of sight for the blind,
To release the oppressed,
To proclaim the Year of The Lord's Favor.
He was telling all who had ears to hear and hearts
to receive that the scripture was fulfilled that day
and his own people did not accept Him
and grew in wrath, threw Him out of the synagogue
escorting Him to a hill. They wanted to throw Him
down headfirst to the ground, but Jesus walked
through the middle of the crowd
and went on His Way.
As the Spirit led Him, He proceeded to preach
in another synagogue being tempted by a man
with an unclean spirit
and cast out devils, performed great miracles
and His Fame was made known throughout.
Whether kneeling, preaching, teaching or healing,
He overcame every fiery dart
confounding the satanic empire
offering Praise and Glory to God
For the Great Things He Had Done.
No greater story ever told in all creation.
The Lord is saying to us
that He has given us the Holy Spirit and
We Are Never Alone,
We Are Never Alone,
We Are Never Alone.

We are complete in Him
if we abide in Him and He abides in us.
Be encouraged for The Lord says:
"Have No Fear
For I am Always Here and Always Near
For this is your season, this is Your Year.
I was born for One Reason
in the APPOINTED SEASON."

Heaven's Gates

There are Mansions in Heaven on streets of gold
with jeweled foundations of precious stone.
Its gates are always open and made of pearl
The nations bringing Glory from around the world
No more curse, no more sorrow
No more worry of tomorrow.
The Lord God as its Temple reigns forevermore.
There are Mansions in Heaven on streets of gold.
Put on garments of valor
and robes of praise
He shall come in His Splendor
and Redeeming Grace
Saying, Enter, O Enter into Heaven's Gates
Reigning with Him forever in His Holy Place.
No more curse, no more sorrow
No more worry of tomorrow.
The Lord God as its Temple reigns forevermore.

Arm of the Lord

He is forever on The Throne
Angels surrounding in Great Song
He sees us when we are sleeping
and in our pain
We lift up our voices without refrain.
Singing Jesus we love You, O Lord we pray
Embrace us in Thy Arms on this Great Day.
We love and adore You
We bow down before You
Offering praises to Your Name.
O, Arm of The Lord,
Extend Your Love
providing for Your People
from Heaven Above.
O, Arm of The Lord
O Arm of The Lord
Forever on Your Throne
in Your Heavenly Home.

Wandering in Darkness

O, Stars of Heaven
Stars of Light
So lovely and bright
That rule by night
You are as spangled garments
Adorned with jewels
That fringe the firmament
Some have lost their brilliance
Some have lost their shine
Has your light gone inward
From the pressures of this Great Time
O, Graveyard of Stars
Wandering in darkness
O, Graveyard of Stars
Wandering in darkness
Extend your spiritual Arm
And be filled with His Brightness
For He is the Star of Bethlehem,
The Bright Morning Star

Spirit of the Lord

The Spirit of The Lord is here
The Spirit of The Lord is here
The Spirit of The Lord is here
Jesus said,
"I must go but I will send The Comforter
He will always be by your side
and He shall abide,
He shall abide within you."
So have no fear, O Child of mine,
For I died for you and many, many others
Who do not even know Me
Tell them that I want to set them free.
Free as a dove,
I send Love from Heaven above
Sing Hallelujah,
Sing Hallelujah, sing Hallelujah
To The Most High God

Turning of the Wall

Changes, changes so many changes
Lord how do we stand
In the midst of so many changes
Are you unctioning
Us to intercede for Your People
Do we dare walk away from this grieving task
Do we pray for the wanderer holding a flask
Do we see beneath the mask
Do we only pray
For those who proclaim to be Christians
Do we choose who we pray for
Do we distinguish between
What we say is good
And what God says is good
Do we seek God in all things
Do we pray to keep chipping away
At that Great Wall
Or do we retreat
Do we not see
The Wall of Protection
Encompassing us
As He gently says,
"Go over the wall, walk in My Trust."

Whisper of the Wind

Do we hear His Small Still Voice?
Hear His Whisper
So, so gentle
The Sweet Whisper of The Wind
The Sweet Whisper of The Wind
O breathe,
O breathe Holy Spirit
Revival throughout the land
What of us does Our Lord command
Revive us, O Lord,
Revive us, O Lord
As we repent and take a stand.

Free at Last

Are you captured
By the beauty of a butterfly
With their wings dancing
If words could be uttered,
You could hear them crying

Free at last,
Free at last,
Free at last.

Let Freedom ring,
And all saints begin to sing,
Freedom is He who dwells in me.

In Memory of Dr. Martin Luther King

The Prize

Are you running the Race?
Can we keep up the Pace?
We walk in His Power and Grace

Pressing on,
Pressing on

To seeing The Son Face to Face

Pressing on,
Pressing on

Longing to dwell in His Holy Place.
Name written down in The Book of Life
His Promise of peace and a New Life
Without strife
So keep running the race
And receive The Prize.

Crack in the Window

As The Son rains Sonlight
Drenched in His Sweetness
As though dripping with honey,
His Love is such a delight
Cleansing tears fall, erasing fears
Little by little
His Blanket of Love destroying doubt
As His Unveiled Truth
u
n
f
o
l
d
s
With a Great Shout.
Jesus is the way
Jesus is the way.
As Life does not announce its next endeavor,
We must go in His Direction
In order to meet Him
Face to Face
As we embrace
His Resting Place.
While watching Him
Orchestrate
His Own Reflection,
His Own Reflection.

Henrietta and Monica

Well, here we are a trio
But we do not know each other
Connected by His Golden Thread
For reasons unknown,
Tears have been prayerfully shed
Lord, lift up my two sisters on this day
On their journey which You have so carefully laid.
Lord, sing a New Song in their lives,
Protecting them from the father of lies
Lord, may their cup runneth over as they hear
I love you,
I love you, My Dear,
I watch over you
as that Great Day is near.

Prayer In Season

At the Sound of the Trumpet

May The Joy of The Lord fill your heart this day.
May you be revived
As that Great Day is approaching
When He will come down from the billowy clouds
As The Trumpet sounds
And His Radiant Light *a-b-o-u-n-d-s*.
The cry of judgment shall be heard
No one will be able to hide by the mountainside
But those who have been righteous in God's sight
Shall meet Him in the air
As they know
He truly cares.
He cares,
He cares,
For us.

Alice

We all stood in your honor yesterday
As we listened intently to your words
I will run again!
Yes, Alice, you will run again.
You will be completely healed.
The Lord is all over you, His Child of Love
He has sent great courage from Heaven Above.
You have touched so many hearts
You are a Miracle
As you read this, listen to His Healing Song
For In Him you are strong
We love you, Alice.

Isaiah 40:31

But they that wait upon The Lord
Shall renew their strength
They shall mount up with wings as eagles
They shall run, and not be weary
And they shall walk, and not faint.

Tears

Many tears, many fears
O, Lord, O Lord erase the fears
To hear, to hear
You saying have no fear.
You are worthy,
You are worthy
To be praised, to be praised,
You are worthy,
You are worthy
To be praised, to be praised
Greatly to be praised
Is Thy Name over all the earth
Angels bow down,
As we wait for our crown,
Witnessing from town to town,
Heaven bound, as we wait for the sound,
The Sound of The Trumpet,
Earth shall pass away,
A New Earth shall appear,
And that Great Day is near,
That Great Day is near.
No more tears, no more fears.

Miracle Over the Mountain

So is the way of the mountain climber
As snow caps the face of an icy hill
Sloping down the valley
As far as the eye can see
Blistering rain promises
A fresh blanket of snow
A warm place can be found
If not alone
Icicles form at nature's best
But the Sun raises its brow
Over the snow caps
Melting nature's picture
Snow-Covered Bliss
O, children, don't miss
The Miracle
Over The Mountain

The Golden Rainbow

Sapphire skies seem to lie as over the horizon
Dances a tormenting storm
But it is not a normal day.
The tormenting rain
Comes as locusts dressed in men's faces
Hidden in the high places
Flooding confusion and brain-crushing pain
Washing many away and due to this,
Jesus says, Walk with the end in mind
As the storm had been allowed,
And at the end of the storm
THE GOLDEN RAINBOW
IN A GOLDEN CLOUD
Will appear,
Brilliantly crystal clear,
Erasing the old, bringing in the new
Skies of purple and royal blue
Bowing before Heaven
Crowning the earth
Reminding you of My Promise
A Crown of Divine Faithfulness
Rainbow Bright,
Orchestrating
My New Day
After
The
Darkest
Night.

Emerald Pools

Purple Dawn awakes
A smiling sunrise partakes
Beckoning the wide-eyed sun
To herald as in a parade
The New Sky in rainbow colors,
The fruitful mountains
In hues of purple and blue,
The bowing trees
Awaiting emerald leaves
And *arched* on a slope.
The Light dancing
Over the emerald pools
Ornate and adorned
As liquid silver jewels
Cascading over blushed mountains
Like a confetti fountain
The grassy meadows *swaying*
In *emeraldic* praise
The valleys facing New Days
A Year of Reaping
And not of Weeping

He Talked to Me Today

Oh, what can I say
About this long awaited
Very special day
He removed all doubt and dismay
I didn't have a clue
As to what He would say or do
He talked to me about each concern
And I laid them down at His Anointed Feet
Issues melted away
As I knelt at the foot of the bed to pray
He made me feel so special
As He talked to me on my level
Preparing the Way
Now as He takes me in His Arms
Please do not be alarmed
As He has brought no shame or harm
He Talked to me today
He Talked to me today
ALWAYS
REMEMBER
HE WILL TALK TO YOU
TODAY.

Thy Heart's Cry

Heal O Lord
The Cries of the Day
Those who are broken
And in dismay
Tell them you love them
Show them the Way,
Thy Faithful Father
Heal them we pray
Touch now Thine afflicted
As we know You do
Love them forever
For Your Heart is True
Anoint Holy Spirit
And Paint Their Sadness
With the Oil of Gladness
Restore them wholly
Mind, Body and Soul
Echoing a New Song
For to You they belong

To Someone

To Someone Who is my friend,
> My Sister in Christ to always be,

To Someone Who helped me
> Along my journey to become free,

To Someone Who is faithful to bend her knee,
> In prayer for her family and whomever it might be.

To Someone Who is in love with The Lord,
> Who loves to read and never gets bored.

To Someone Who has unconditional love,
> And the angels surround from above.

To Someone That always lends a listening ear,
> And oftentimes out of compassion sheds loving tears.

To Someone Who encourages as many as She meets and
> Who lies lovingly at Jesus' Precious feet.

To Someone Who is truly genuine as well as sweet,
> Who loves to eat, and who is like no other that I will ever meet.

TO MY SISTERS IN CHRIST

Songbird

O, Wounded Soldier,
Speak to the torment of the night
No longer will your emptiness satisfy me
"Blame it on the poison
Blame it on the poison," whispered The Songbird.
With a wide-eyed gaze,
He did drink from the sun-kissed horizon
As Love was shining a New Song
"O, Heaven, Such Joy, what is that I hear? He said.
I listen intently as I rehearse with The Songbird
Who has perched on my windowsill
Reminding me that
The Arm of The Lord is close at hand.
Sing, Sing, Sing His Healing Song
His Return From Heaven won't be long."

Kiss

Early in the morning you wake us with a kiss
Telling us to rise up for another day of bliss.
The flowers moistened by the morning dew
Dancing into blossom before the day is through.
We scurry around to meet the needs of our loved ones
In hopes that we will get it all done.
We wear many masks as we endeavor to do our daily tasks,
But in all that we do
We give thanks for Your Amazing Grace
Which pulls us through.
Dear Lord when Night draws near
We can still hear Your Voice saying,
"Have no fear for I am here."
We close our joyful eyes
With thoughts of love
As You watch over us
From Heaven above

Coffee, Tea or Me

When you gaze at this special gift
Sit down and sip of Me
Let your spirit soar
As I have blessings galore
A new door refreshing and clean
Now let Me tell you what this all means
My cup overflowing
Filled with new ground,
New beginning topsoil
More joy less toil.
My fragrance engaged
As though surrounding you within a cage.
Extra benefits are in store
Now let Me tell you more.
The enemy will be at bay
New Beginning, New Day.
I will answer before you ask
My Labor
Not your task.
A
RIBBON
OF
PROMISE.

Scratch My Wings

"Scratch My Wings"
Oh, Anointed One,
My Everlasting King
Three words that will continually ring
In expectation of the comfort
You will faithfully bring.
Make my heart sing
As You deliver Your Messages
One by one
Thank you for the added plus
As in my life
The Holy Angels are a must.
I long for others to know You as I do
Open their knowledge and understanding
That as The Angels ministered to You
They can be ministered to.
So Scratch my wings, Lord,
As You lighten the load
And make me
Whiter than snow
And as pure gold

The Sandy Rose

The morning dew fell causing a light glaze
The rising of the Sun orchestrating the day,
And it was not an ordinary day
But a day to be purged
Of the previous day's sorrow
Much had The Lord done to bring joy
Into each tomorrow
And had encouraged
The desert to bloom
Like a fragrant rose
Only God knows the destiny
That He has chosen
For each of us
From beginning to end
So allow Him to mend
All the broken places

New Day Dawning

There is a new day dawning
A Brighter Tomorrow
Put on a garment of joy
And remove the garment of sorrow.
Our trust is in The Lord
So as you watch Him take up His Sword
To subdue all of your enemies
Wait to hear Him say as He did to David,
"I have subdued all of your enemies.
I have placed you in a large place
See all of The Angels I have sent
Shining all around you like jewels
They are closer than you think
And move on your behalf as quickly as a wink."

The Late Night Watchman

Who do you go to when no one is around
But to Jesus Christ having been transformed to a higher ground
Not earth as we know it but according to Heaven's worth.
Christ was before everything and became a part of creation
And then returned to eternity. Can we understand.
No we can't.
Everything that we do is done in and through Christ.
We have no ability to change ourselves in any way
With any degree representing a true miracle.
We are in His Hands if we would just stay there.
And even in that, He is faithful to His Word,
To never leave us nor forsake us in sickness and in health,
In well doing and in not so well doing,
In going in and in going out,
In day-to-day.
The key here is that Christ died for all situations,
For all types of people
And for every single moment of our lives
It's because of Him that we live today.
Mankind would have totally destroyed itself except that the
Bible holds true to the fact that The Holy Ghost
Was sent to earth
To encompass the whole earth
As a "Watchman."
Angels know not the hour
But they are obedient to Our Lord,
A Great fragrant flower
That refreshes after a stormy shower
As the beautiful rainbow
Dances in praise in a multicolored array
Promising
A
BRIGHTER DAY.

The Jewel's Vine

A stitch in time saves nine
A setting without a jewel
Is like a grape without a vine.
We were born to draw all men unto Him
To some people we are the only Light they will see
So in ministering to them how hard could it be.
You say I'm saved and sanctified
Whose voice have you heard
What choice have you made
Too, too many are out there
Wandering with eyes in a hopeless glaze
May The Lord set you ablaze
And reveal to you in a very personal way
That He is
The Truth, The Life and The Way
Follow Him
He is The True Vine
The Jewel's Vine

John 15:1:

*Jesus said, "I am the true vine,
and My Father is the vinedresser."*

Precious Jewels to Behold

For what price have you been sold
The price of Truth is that you embrace The Vine
As The Vine embraces You.
His Thoughts towards you are that
He longs to talk and walk
With you as Your True Friend
Stating that He will be with you
Before the beginning and until the end
A precious stone
With a face crystal clear
A stone mounted on High
Worshipping its Maker
Who looks low from On High
A servant in the truest sense of the word
Giving all of Himself
Sharing His secrets and His Wealth

My Tablet

My Tablet
My Ever Present Help
My Plan, My Answer
My Tablet vs. your tablet
Who can compare how precious it is
To be given the answer as soon as you ask
For leaning on your own answer is no easy task.
Jesus has His Plan for our destiny
Creatively mapped out
So lift up your voice and SHOUT
His Plan, His Answer is what it is all about.
Your tablet cannot compare to His Tablet
For on it He has written an answer
For every concern,
Every situation, every hurt,
Every tear and every fear

His Word tells us to:

*"Be of good cheer for
He has overcome the world."*

As you look at The Book take a closer look
and see that it is His Tablet
The source for having all our needs met.

God's Blueprint

He looked down from His Heavenly Home. Much is unknown about His Heavenly Home as His Word tells us that we will know in part. The world was a dark and barren sketch. A raw spiritual picture. An ever evolving sketch. A blueprint in the making. The Heavenly Bodies, the lands enveloped in salty blue seas and waters, with the topaz sky kissing the high and low lands. The magnetic force in and of itself a wonder to behold. The wind was unseen but not forgotten – a great marvel. There were changing of the Seasons and atmosphere with the sun and moon sharing the spotlight. Stars dancing around throughout the night dazzling with their twinkling lights. He created a place for habitation of different types. Life as we know it: the plant life, the animal life, the sea life, the bird life and the bug life. Different textures, different colors and both pleasant and unpleasant fragrances. All created for a purpose in mind.

He had a plan.
He had a purpose.

> When man was created from the dust of the earth,
> God created him in His Own Image.
> His most prized and precious plan and purpose of all.

We are here because
God did not want to be alone.

Flecks of Gold

Such grace to behold
As whispering angels unfold
Ministering to the Young,
And the Old
Appearing when least expected
And hoping we won't be affected
By their Presence
Except to bring Honor and Glory to God.
Gabriel appeared to Mary,
A devout woman
Speaking of a Child of Love.
An Angel appeared to Joseph
Speaking about the Virgin Child
And about Mary
Removing any suspicion or doubt
He had to the contrary.
Jacob wrestled with an angel
All night
With all of his might
Wonder who won the fight?
A New Name to claim
And the old nature in flames.

He is the Cornerstone

Jesus is the Cornerstone
The Walls are built by Him Alone
Foundation Sure
Of Gold and Pure
Because of Him we can endure.
Jesus is the Cornerstone
The walls are built by Him alone
Foundation Sure
Of Gold and Pure
Because of Him we can endure.
We are God's people
We are God's people
We are building the walls on a firm foundation
He was nailed to the cross for our salvation
We lift up our voices in celebration
With eyes lifted up in adoration
We are God's People
We are God's People.

Breath of Heaven

In Heaven we have a Blessing Tree
And our surrendered love
Is the cost or fee
From this tree
Fall the
D
E
W
D
R
O
P
S
As though Heaven
Is crying along with us
And as though they never stop.

GOD'S LOVE
NEVER
STOPS.

For Such a Time as This

You did not pray amiss
As you walk and talk with Him
He will show you where you are
And where you have been
The Bible, our Living Book
Gives us His Promise,
More than just a look
With Him we will always WIN!
He is brighter than a Star,
But He is close as well as far,
He is a Shining Light
To erase the darkest night
Some fine Glorious day
He will come with the angels
Trumpeting and resounding His Fury
Against the enemy at hand
Can't you just see Him
Won't it be grand!

Such Joy as we connect with our Risen King,

Such gladness of heart freedom can bring,

With Joy overflowing and full of Glory,

Embracing His Love as we tell His Story.

Seek His Face

Enter the Throne of Grace
Petition and seek His Face
He's Alpha,
Omega
And on The Throne
Letting you know
You're not alone.
He answers prayer
He's always there
His Majestic Throne
You're not alone
Find your place
Seek His Face
Seek His Face.
His Majestic Throne
For Kingdom's Sake
So please partake
His Kingdom come
Thy will be done.

The Spirit's Blessing

A star was born
One Christmas morn
The skies were singing virgin birth
The earth rejoice
God made His Choice
The Spirit's Blessing through Mary
Angels dancing
Three wisemen glancing
With gifts
frankincense, gold and myrrh
While they're glancing
They are proclaiming
This Child has come
To save the earth.

Step by Step

Praise to Our Heavenly Father
His Name is Jesus,
Teach us to pray
Shape us and mold us
As we walk along the way.
Guide us into
All Truth and Goodness
So we may then soar
And by yielding to Your Spirit
We can endure.
Step by step
Lord
We look to Thee
Seeking Your Mercy
While knelt on our knees.

Valley of Peace

As I stepped out of an air-conditioned building, it was as though I had stepped into another world, unknown, but I did know this world —The Valley of Peace. I could hear Heaven crying "Peace, Peace, Peace." As I stepped down the stairs and walked into the sun, the sun pleasingly danced around me. It was as though the Son had enveloped me totally.

I noticed the other voices trying to harmonize with this delightful cry. There were voices of birds, cows, traveling cars and people scurrying to their next destination. I thanked The Lord for the one cry, Peace, which subdued all of the other voices. The troubles of the day could have been another voice but that voice could not be heard. At that very moment, the one cry became the only cry.

"Peace be still and know I am God."
Peace in the midst of a storm.

Silent Smile

Well, Lord, you are ministering to me in many areas in a mighty way. Truth unfolds in each spiritual lesson. At the moment, my thoughts center on when you told me you would clear up the confusion. Yes, you are. There seems to be more light in the tunnel. Boy, am I glad I don't have to go through the tunnel by myself! As I think about the word "tunnel", I think of the word "narrow."

> *"Narrow is the Way and broad is the road that leads to destruction."*

Narrow is a straight path with His protection around us pointing in His Direction. He has His Arms open wide. Can you hear Him saying, *"My Daughter, My Son, you can make it. You can make it."* I feel Your Presence as though You are prompting each word. How do I describe. An intimacy with You, Your Love at hand, a gift that You are cultivating so it can be shared with others. Oh Lord, that others could write out those un-vented feelings. My husband is watching television, but he cannot give to me what I am experiencing right now. I am experiencing Peace, fulfillment and all needs have been met. The expression on my face has become a silent smile that you understand. In You, I am placed above my circumstances. Your Ways are hard to understand but Your Love is too hard to turn away from. You are able to hold us in Your Hand. You have been talking to me about relationships - detach. Let go and Let God.

You have given me food and water to sustain me through this desert experience and not too soon. I thought that I was going to have a heat stroke! Oh gee, the devil lost again.

> *"As a deer panteth for the water So my soul panteth after Thee."*

I Am With You in Spirit

"*Except that I go, The Comforter cannot come,*" said Jesus as He ascended into Heaven. The disciples were astounded, and they did not understand why He could not be with them any longer. But soon, The Comforter descended to fill the broken hearts of those who longed for His Presence. Joy unspeakable and full of Glory permeated the entire room. The disciples prayed and sang in The Spirit, lifting up their voices of praise unto Him who is able to keep them from falling. We live in a beautiful time, great signs and wonders to behold.

What does He have in store for His Children?

As we walk in the beauty of The Lord, we feel His touch
As though we are wrapped in a warm blanket,
Saturated in His Love and never wanting to leave.

Peace, Peace, Peace. Let your heart ring with Peace.

The Uncertainties in Witnessing

Lord, it is hard to understand, probably impossible to understand why so many people have such a hard time believing in You. You walked this earth and many, many people did not believe in You when You were here in the flesh! It hurts, Lord. I grieve as You must have grieved. It really hurts.

Lord, You send us out to touch lives and we do not know what to expect sometimes, but Your Word does not return void. Naturally people do not understand but Your Word is still true. Thank You for The Comforter whom I am falling in love with Lord. You fulfilled Your Promise when You told the disciples that You had to leave but You would send The Comforter. Learning about all the experiences You had is a very painful process.

Your goodness cannot be quenched. Give us boldness to continue Lord knowing that we might receive a harsh or angry response. The world says You can talk a little bit about Jesus but not too much. If it makes the world uncomfortable, they will let you know. Isolation is an evil spirit that tries to convince believers that they should keep their light under a bushel or hidden.

> You say, *"You are The Light of the world*
> *Go out and witness as unto Me. I will be with Thee."*

Thank You Lord for being with us, for interceding for us. You really have never left us. You are very much alive and moving in Your Church today. I cannot wait until I come face to face with You and feel all of Your Love in its fullness.

THANK YOU LORD. THANK YOU LORD.

Nothing Can Keep Me Down

Lord, thank you for the words piercing my heart. Words in a sermon prepared especially for Your people, Your chosen Ones. The Pastor delivered a sermon that I would entitle 'Nothing can keep me down'. The story was about Joseph. What a story to read! God had shown him in a dream that he would reign over many, but the dream took years to materialize. What Joseph experienced, he came out on top because Jesus was at the forefront.

Is Jesus at the forefront in our lives?

I did not realize how much these words would minister to me, until the next day when I had to experience firsthand a very difficult situation. This situation became silent because The Word came forth with such vitality and truth.

Thank You Lord—You always know what we need to hear.

City Lights

O, Peace of Night
You are like
The pureness of angels in flight
City Lights,
Ordained by God's Command
To meet a sleeper's demand.
A sleeper's delight
With fire by night
And seemingly no worries in sight
A mighty rushing wind
Assigned to win
As well as defend
At day's end

Embrace Me

Please embrace me,
Please embrace me, Lord
Please embrace me
As I dance before Your Throne
Giving honor
Giving praise
Giving glory
To Your Holy Name
I love You,
I adore You,
And I bow down before You
I worship You, I worship You, I worship You
I worship You, I worship You, I worship You
Please embrace me,
Please embrace me,
Please embrace me.
Cover me with Your Love, Lord
Sing to me with the voice of an angel

Turning Your Home Into a Fortress

In August 1990, The Lord gave me a specific prayer:

"Pray that Angels will be encamped about
and continually sing praises
Walls will sing out praises
The ceiling will rain down righteousness
The windows will cry out for mercy
The carpet will cry out love to all
Pictures will draw serenity
(clear and free of any unpleasant
change or storms)
Furniture will bring Holy Ghost Conviction
The water will run in a continuous stream
The Lights will turn on for joy and peace
and the dishes will cry out hunger for God's Word."

Middle of the Road

Trust in Me and I will set you free
Go the road as I carry the load
Follow and seek
And I will make you meek
Trust,
Go
And
Follow Me.
Tell the devourer to come no more
As I close that ugly, fearful door
New doors will swing open
And I am whom you place your hope in.
"Angels fear to tread
And so by Him they are lead"
Or so you have read
I am Your Daily Bread.
"Middle of the Road" is an ugly term,
Or so it would seem
But I am your light,
Your Everlasting beam
Which gleans over a flowing stream
Which pours out of your dreams.
You could be in the "Middle" of sin
Or imprisoned in a lion's den
Wondering when will this nightmare end…
So as you write this in pen
Know that My Small Still Voice is heard again.

I Kings 19:11-12

Then He said, "Go out and stand on the mountain before the Lord." And Behold, the Lord passed by, and a great and strong wind tore into the mountains and broke the rocks in pieces before the Lord, but the Lord was not in the wind; and after the wind an earthquake, but the Lord was not in the earthquake; and after the earthquake a fire, but the Lord was not in the fire, and after the fire a small still voice.

Birthday Present

O, Lord,
O Lord,
How I have longed for this day,
My Birthday
A day blessed by You
My desires have come true.

O, thank You Lord,
O thank You Lord,
You touched my heart,
Renewed my mind,
Changed my attitude,
And increased my faith and joy.
I surrendered,
I surrendered.

And then
You ever
So graciously
Took control.

I couldn't ask for anything more,
But Lord I do want more
I want more and more and more of You
Thank You for Your
Amazing Grace,
Amazing Grace,
Amazing Grace,
Amazing Grace.

Majestic Beauty

In our meekness
God promoted time after time
So as you are captured
By the majestic beauty
Of the mountain,
Be reminded of the mountain
You had
To climb
But you were not alone.
He provided the way
Speaking to you
In a soft hushed tone
Saying,
*"You are not alone
I am with you."*

Hiding Place

The wounds go deep, Lord,
To what can I afford
The trials of the day
Coming to steal my joy away.
My heart hurts, Lord,
What about that?
Do I go into combat
Or do I hide
As in You I do abide.
Lord, please be my hiding place
And get the devil off my case
As I seek Your Face.

Out of Prayer

We have a notion
We have a theory
Entering each day
Without prayer
Should make one leery.
For each day that begins
That we fail to enter in
Many of us go about the day
In dismay
This is not meant to be condemnation
But rather revelation
A day starting and ending in peace
His Direction
He will release.
In Prayer, He will inspire
Talking to us about every desire
And His words will comfort
And take us up higher.
Our thoughts will become His thoughts
Our desires will become His Desires
He will always inspire.
Day to day can drag us down
Not knowing which way to turn
But may this be a lesson to learn
Without prayer
You will be burned.
Prayer keeps the enemy at bay
Sending him in seven different ways
The enemy has no place in our lives
Except to kill, destroy and tell lies.
What does he do? He starts rumors and wars

But we have Jesus,
Our Great and Magnificent Star.
He never leaves us nor forsakes us
But He is jealous
As He knows
The enemy is relentless
During a winter season,
I say winter as I was not myself,
I grew very depressed
And The Lord said, *"Depression is not real."*
Happily I knew that this winter season was about to close.
No one knows
Except Jesus what can enter the mind
Of a person who is depressed
Everything as they know it becomes a total mess.
They will turn to other people
It's almost as though they forgot or don't feel worthy
To enter God's temple
The entrance to His altar is lovingly open
Enter in for He is Who to place your hope in.
To my amazement, He always provides
A way of escape
In that dark hour
He drew me closer
And I offered a sweet fragrance
To Him in prayer
As a wilted flower
You may be weary
You may be tired
Lift up your petition
And as a person climbs a stair
On His Throne
You will surely find Him there.
He prays to The Father

For every condition
Offer a sweet fragrance
To Him in prayer
As a wilted flower
Just One Word from God
Can change
Night Into Day
Fright Into His Insight
Tears
Into
Knowing
He Hears.

In Prayer

Enter in
He surrounds with an invisible shield
Just yield, just yield.
His sweet fragrance He brings
You may hear a ringing
As though
Heaven's chime
Was clinging.
Oh such joy to feel
As He becomes so, so real
The tick of a clock doesn't mean anything to Him
Around the clock He prays
Take your shoes off, enter in and stay.
He lends an ear
He's always clear,
He's always near.
After asking for His forgiveness,
You have a clean slate
It is never too late.
You have heard that God is always on time
He has our best interest at heart
Pull at His Heartstrings
And forever to His Bosom cling
Enter in
Hear the ring of Heaven's chime
One
More
Time.

The Master's Touch

No need to pretend
Some days we can't wait until the day ends
But a New Day always begins
In Christ you are a winner
And He will always defend.
Sometimes we neglect to pray
And a bad situation knocks us down
Reach for His Hand and He will pull you up
May His Love fill your cup
There is no other place that we can go
To receive so much
Than when receiving the Master's Touch
Joy overflowing
A face lit up and glowing
Living Water flowing
A continuous stream gleaming
To erase the tears
That are sometimes streaming.
As you glance towards Heaven today
See the windows of Heaven opening up wide
To welcome you into His Glorious Light
Darkness has no place in His Sight
Jesus loves us so much
Feel
The Master's Touch.

Draw from the Fountain

Jesus said, "If I be lifted up, I will all men unto me." "Taste and drink

DRAW
FROM
THE
FOUNTAIN

He has made provision, a well of living water that never runs dry, healing virtue descending from the sky, my, my, my! Draw from His Strength as He will go to any length. No greater love has He than for you and me. He is the Potter and we are the clay. He knows the beginning and the end. His Living Word tells us "all things work together for the good to those who are called according to His Purpose." Purpose do we know what purpose is? We are each a unique piece of clay and surely according to His Purpose, there will be no delay. Purpose is a step-by-step process as He guides along the way. There are desert-like seasons that seem to come out of nowhere and yet He always provides a way of escape. He wrote our book of life.

Fill each day of your life

DRAW FROM THE FOUNTAIN.

Express One's Gratitude

There are no words to fully express one's gratitude
When The Lord has changed one's attitude
Removing doubt, anger and a tendency to be rude.
There is a completely different spiritual mood.
Weights have been lifted,
The direction has shifted,
Mind has become clear
With Jesus at the center and very near
If you were doubting or pouting,
One Word from Jesus
Can change miraculously
Into a Great Shout
The expression
"Sticks and stones will break my bones,
But words will never hurt me."
Jesus is our foundation,
Our rock, our stepping stone
In Him
You will not stand alone

Express your Gratitude

Fragranced Home

Blessings each day
A warm place to stay
With His Fragrance permeating the room
Removing all gloom.
A day should be filled with early prayer
Kneeling down or maybe sitting in a chair
He will not give us more than we can bear.
More than we can bear, comforting words
For us to hear as we draw near
God knows what we need
Even before we ask
He is always willing to offer His Help
For each task
If you lack knowledge, He will give it to you
If you need a shoulder to cry on, He will hold you
If you are riding a storm, He will guide you
If you this, if you that,
In whatever you lack
He will be there to pick up the slack.
He will offer His Sweet Fragrance
For the time you spent with Him
Start Now
Just Begin.

Protection Bottle

There is a day
There is a night
Angels in flight
Day or night
In all their diligence and might.
You may not see them
But they are always there
Following Jesus who gives the command
That all mankind be watched over in the land.
On land, in the air or by sea
They are everywhere watching over you and me.
We worship Our Savior who lovingly sends them forth
East, West, South and to the North
Take a moment to thank The Lord for His Added protection
And lift up your voice in angelic selection
We are God's elect and His delight
He will never leave us or be out of our sight.
East, West, South and North
His Angels have been sent forth
In all directions
Make Jesus your choice today,
Your selection!

About the Author

A beautiful poetic journey to walk in the beauty of The Lord and to be encouraged as The Lord inspired this writer. A Gift with His Plan and His Purpose to be shared with others. On June 26, 1990 during a time of study, The Lord inspired Cheryl to write down certain scriptures in her journal that were referring to the poets in the bible. Several months later, the first poem 'The Rose' was inspired. A rose goes through many seasons. The rose bud, the rose blossom and the sandy rose Writings continue as The Lord inspires. Throughout the years, the collection of poems has been shared with many people in all walks of life.

Cheryl was born in Belleville, Illinois and her family moved to California when she was fourteen. In high school, creative writing was a chore. She didn't have any desire to write. Then fourteen years later, She accepted Jesus as her personal Savior and everything changed. Today She loves writing and looks forward to each inspired poem. As The Lord has encouraged Cheryl with each one, may He encourage each one of You.

Cheryl raised a daughter, two sons, and has been blessed with nine grandchildren. In addition to spiritual writing, She enjoys collecting angels, home decorating and the Drama Ministry.

www.ingramcontent.com/pod-product-compliance
Lightning Source LLC
LaVergne TN
LVHW041629070526
838199LV00052B/3294